HOW TO
Be A Villain

EVIL LAUGHS SECRET LAIRS
Master Plans And More!!!

by neil zawacki

illustrations | **james dignan**

CHRONICLE BOOKS
SAN FRANCISCO

Sincerest thanks to everyone who helped with this book, especially Shannon, without whom none of this would have been possible.

Library of Congress Cataloging-in Publication Data available.

ISBN: 0-8118-4666-0

Manufactured in China

Design by BC Design
www.bcdesign.com

Distributed in Canada by Raincoast Books
9050 Shaughnessy Street
Vancouver, British Columbia V6P 6E5

10 9 8 7 6 5 4 3 2

Chronicle Books LLC
85 Second Street
San Francisco, California 94105

www.chroniclebooks.com

Contents

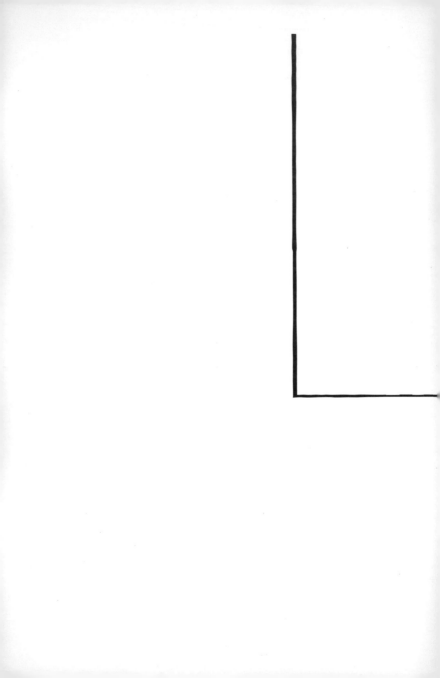

This book is dedicated to everyone who ever thought evil was just a dream. Rejoice, would-be miscreants, your time has come!

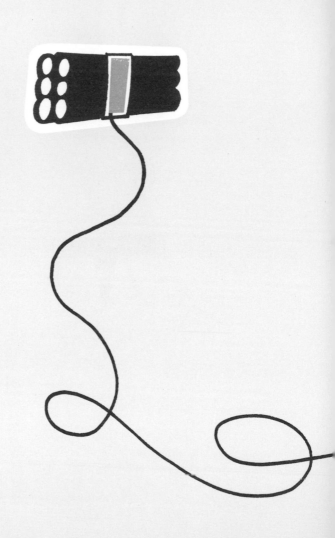

Chapter

Getting Started with the Forces of Darkness

"If you only knew the power of the Dark Side..."   — *Darth Vader*

Congratulations on your decision to join the forces of darkness... Evil can always use another talented agent to lend a hand in the name of mayhem. The sooner you get started, the sooner you can enjoy the fruits of limitless power, revel in unbridled greed and debauchery, and begin the construction of the enormous and needlessly complex weapons of destruction in your basement.

Whether you practice evil in the privacy of your own home or set your goals at nothing less than international domination, you'll find plenty of valuable tips in this guide. Whatever your background or experience, rest assured there's an aspect of evil that's right for you. If you don't find your niche immediately, don't despair. This handy guide is designed to help you discover and nurture the darkness within for a lifetime of heedless villainy. No matter how well adjusted you may appear to friends and family, you are the only one who can truly know your evil potential.

TIP: If you find that you still lack confidence, try this exercise. Stand in front of a mirror with the lights turned off. Stare at your ghostly visage and say with confidence, "I'm bad. I'm really, really bad."

Evil deeds don't need to be catastrophic to be rewarding. Indeed, plenty of minor acts can be satisfyingly unpleasant. Start small and work your way up to more infamous exploits. Here are a few ideas:

- **Realign the moon's orbit (you can always do Earth later)**
- **Turn a popular landmark into a gelatinous ooze**
- **Release a demonic hoard on a peaceful township**
- **Learn to play the pipe organ and volunteer at church functions**
- **Broadcast your evil plans on public access television**

Remember, most of the mightily evil people you admire today probably failed once or twice along the way. Part of being evil is having the courage to keep on trying, even if your sinister shenanigans don't always inspire terror and strife.

The Concept of Evil

The first step in an evil education is to understand the true meaning of the term. The dictionary offers one definition:

Evil (adj.) 1. Having qualities tending to injury and mischief; having a nature or properties which tend to badness; mischievous; not good; worthless or deleterious; poor; as, an evil beast, an evil plant, an evil crop. 2. Having or exhibiting bad moral qualities; morally corrupt; wrong; vicious; as, evil conduct, thoughts, heart, words, and the like.

There is more, but you probably get the point. Evil is anarchy. Evil is lawless. Evil is wicked. But isn't there more to it than that? Yes, what the dictionary cleverly leaves out is for an elect few to know: Evil is fun.

The Benefits of Being Evil

Being evil is more than a job, it's a lifestyle. By embracing the dark forces, otherwise ordinary men, women, and even children and pets can gain power and wealth beyond their wildest dreams. Perhaps the single greatest benefit of a career in evil is equal access to executive level positions. Black, white, or green; male, female, or alien life form; spikes, scales, or brain in a jar—nothing prevents a devotee of darkness from rising to the top of the quagmire of destruction.

Power and wealth are not the only benefits. Servants of darkness, despite the secondary role that name implies, also enjoy deliciously unrestricted creative freedom. Evil knows no boundaries. If you can dream an evil plot, you can do it—and become a ray of darkness in an otherwise unbearably sunny day.

Evil careers offer extensive supernatural benefits, too. Many evil-doers develop the ability to manifest themselves wherever and whenever they choose. For those who excel, there is even the possibility of immortality.

In the end, the most important part of being evil is feeling good about your bad self. Only then will you walk down the street with pride, smiling broadly as small children in your path abandon their favorite playthings and flee as though approached by a swarm of locusts.

Although it's possible to be evil in any vocation, certain careers practically force you to exploit your dark side. Your best bets:

- **Night manager of a deserted warehouse**
- **Mad scientist**
- **Shape-shifter**
- **Voodoo princess**
- **Slave driver**
- **Orc, ogre, or zombie**
- **Telemarketer**

Careers in Evil

Become a ray of darkness in an otherwise unbearably sunny day.

Am I Evil?

Do you have what it takes to be deeply and disturbingly evil? Complete this quick quiz to find out.

How do you start your morning?

A. Rise at six, shower while humming chipper tune
B. Perform vigorous knee bends and enjoy bracing five-mile jog
C. Hit the snooze alarm until hopelessly late for work
D. Sip a cup of coffee, read the newspaper, plot the downfall of civilization

Which of the following best describes your talents?

A. People person
B. Manager
C. Multitasker
D. Snake charmer

What did you want to be when you grew up?

A. Police officer
B. Doctor
C. Ballerina
D. Supreme dark overlord of all mankind, or a lawyer

Do you have any pets?

A. Puppy
B. Bird
C. Iguana
D. An aquarium filled with piranhas, electric eels, and killer sharks

How do you normally spend your weekends?

A. Hiking mountain trails
B. Watching television
C. Hanging out with friends
D. Constructing doomsday devices in the basement

What torments you in your worst nightmares?

A. A fiery building from which I cannot escape
B. Monsters with huge teeth
C. Vengeful ex-lovers
D. Unicorns, rainbows, and puppy dogs with soulful eyes

What are your religious beliefs?

A. Christian, Jewish, Muslim
B. Buddhist, Hindu, pagan
C. Atheist or agnostic
D. I am actually an ancient Babylonian god awoken from a terrible sleep

What would you say is the greatest threat to society today?

A. Crime, drugs, and gangs
B. Multinational corporations
C. Nuclear war
D. Me

What is your reaction when confronted by a crucifix or holy water?

A. Feel the divine light surround your spiritual aura
B. Contemplate how far civilization has come
C. Chuckle at their ridiculous superstitious beliefs
D. Run away while screaming "It burns! It burns!"

It's the end of the world. An atomic blast has just leveled the cities and destroyed the human race. Mutants walk the streets and the seas have boiled away to nothing. Civilization as you know it is over. What do you do?

A. Vow to someday rebuild society
B. Double over in grief and wait for a merciful death
C. Try to remember the plot to *The Road Warrior*
D. Congratulate yourself on a job well done

Answers

Tally up your answers by counting the number of times each letter was connected to your responses.

Mostly As, Bs, or Cs: Unfortunately you do not possess the necessary qualities to be a supervillain. Please continue exploring your inner evil and try again next year.

Mostly Ds: Excellent. You are predestined to menace society.

Choosing an Evil Name

To get your evil career launched with flair, you'll want to choose an evil name for yourself. A good one is memorable, pithy, and conjures up images of endless torment. A short name is generally preferable, especially since you will want to carve it into stone, have it tattooed on all of your servants, and emblazon it on your armor and weaponry. Choose carefully, because this is what the world will know you as throughout time, and once it's out there in the zeitgeist, it's hell getting the thing changed.

TIP: Many great names are already taken but can be modified to good use, such as Satan's Handyman or Mistress of the Dark Prince.

the normal name This is where you keep your current name and simply use that in your quest for ultimate evil. Believe it or not, you don't *always* need a big flash name—it just helps. Trust in your evil deeds, and, should you become terrible enough, that alone can be enough to inspire fear in all humanity. Examples include Bill Gates, Pat Robertson.

the descriptive name Like a tag line in brand marketing, a descriptive name lets people know immediately something about you and what makes you different. Gather friends and family and brainstorm to discover the key element of your evil identity. What makes you so bad? If you like to crush things, for example, you might decide to call yourself The Pulverizer. Evil geniuses with multiple limbs might opt for The Octopus, and Eater of Souls is always good for destroyers of humanity. While you are brainstorming, don't shoot down an idea just because it's not exactly right. Even the silliest suggestion might lead to a wonderfully sinister name later.

Countess Carnal

the sinister name Want more options in the evil lexicon? The following chart will help you come up with a name sure to cause millions to tremble. To create a name worthy of your destructive tendencies, simply select one word from each column and combine the words in columns two and three. For example, you might try on Baron Bloodspawn for size. Don't limit yourself to the suggestions printed here. If you can think of more evil terms on your own, add them to the chart. Then mix, match, and let your creativity blossom.

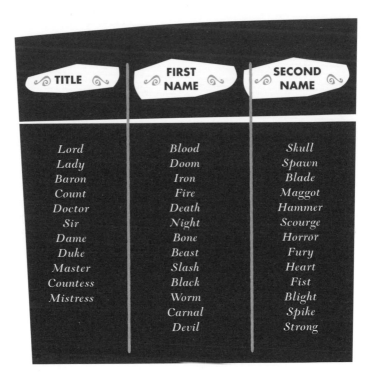

TITLE	FIRST NAME	SECOND NAME
Lord	Blood	Skull
Lady	Doom	Spawn
Baron	Iron	Blade
Count	Fire	Maggot
Doctor	Death	Hammer
Sir	Night	Scourge
Dame	Bone	Horror
Duke	Beast	Fury
Master	Slash	Heart
Countess	Black	Fist
Mistress	Worm	Blight
	Carnal	Spike
	Devil	Strong

Make your new designation echo in the minds of the timid for eons with a sophisticated brand name. You won't need to consult Madison Avenue; chances are, you can come up with great ideas on your own. An effective evil branding may include any or all of the following:

Evil Branding

SLOGAN ◄ Three to five words that sum up your evil ways in an intimidating fashion. Remember, you're talking directly to your victims, so make your message something they can relate to, such as *"Mercy Is Not an Option!"*

JINGLE ◄ Jingles are memorable, contagious, and easier to invent than you think. Select a song you like and change the words to describe yourself.

LOGO (monstrous skulls, deadly scorpions, and pyramids with eyes) ◄ Iconic representation is a must these days, plus it gives you an artful way to leave your mark in the wake of destruction.

TRADEMARK GESTURE ◄ Whether you leave behind a token of your villainy or howl from a mountaintop each fortnight, consistent delivery of a gesture or symbolic act, in other words a trademark, will help reinforce your name and identity, making it that much more likely that your evil ways will survive in perpetuity.

LITERARY LEGACY ◄ If a legacy of evil is important to you, be sure to find your way into fables, lore, literature, song, and even film. What better way to attain evil stature than by starring in your own major motion picture?

Create a Jingle

Jingles help people remember your name long after you've moved on to menace other territories. Here's an easy formula for success, even if you've never written an evil jingle before.

STEP ONE ◄ State who you are.
I'm Barstil the wing-ed succubus,

STEP TWO ◄ Rhyming on the last syllable of line one, elaborate on one of your qualities.
I'm way more than egre-gi-ous.

STEP THREE ◄ State what you like to do.
I'll eat you up and spit you out,

STEP FOUR ◄ Rhyming on the last syllable of line three, state the consequences or result of your action.
You'll wish your affliction was merely gout!

Mercy Is Not an Option!

Make your message something they can relate to.

Motives

The next step toward creating your evil persona is to consider your motive. Why do you do the things you do? Is it the power? The money? The glory? Or are you just bad to the bone? Evil comes from many sources; here are just a handful.

power A prime motivator, the lust for power fuels many a malcontent. Power lets you do anything you want while remaining completely unaccountable for your actions. Do you feel the overwhelming desire to crush all beneath your might and control all that exists? If so, you're probably motivated by a strong affinity for power. Total supremacy is, of course, very tempting and explains why power has remained the top driving force among evil-doers for millennia.

Unmitigated greed is often an expedient route to nastiness.

greed Many observers see greed as a superior motive to both power and hate, because it typically leads to *wealth* and *material riches*. This is not to say that it in any way impedes the pursuit of evil; in fact, quite the contrary. Unmitigated greed, which often includes exploitation, theft, and wholesale corruption, is often an expedient route to nastiness. Due to the typically high profit margin of evil deeds, amassing an evil fortune can be remarkably quick and easy.

hate Many evil-doers are motivated by a strong hatred for all mankind. They want nothing more than to punish anyone who has ever committed the unforgivable crime of having been born. Evil-doers with this motivation are usually predisposed to venomous wrath and mindless rage, and will often rain down destruction even at the cost of their own lives. Though constant stress is an unfortunate side effect, hatred can be a truly magnificent force to behold.

insanity Many evil-doers have been propelled to greatness through insanity. Some hear voices in their heads, others can't tell right from wrong. Whatever your particular derangement, insanity is, by definition, incredibly disturbing both to you and those around you. As such, you may want to consider losing your mind before embarking on your evil career, so as not to be inconvenienced by your own madness. Madness scores high for originality and can direct you in ways normally thought impossible, or not thought at all, because they're, well, insane.

revenge Another favorite, revenge is the extreme desire to *make them pay,* whomever they may be. Try to think of something unpleasant that happened to you in the past. Chances are, you can find someone to blame for this agony. Did the other children torment you for being "different"? Did your teachers say you'd never amount to any kind of genius, evil or not? They deserve to pay dearly. You suffered, why shouldn't they? If this logic makes sense to you, then you are motivated by revenge. Or maybe you're just really, really petty. Whatever the case, never let go of your resentment over past injuries. Mull them over daily, if necessary, because without anger, you are nothing.

evil, it's my nature For some wrongdoers, evil is not sought. Rather, it's inherent to their being. When a child is born with glowing red eyes and strange cloven hooves it is not too unusual for them to discover evil as their true calling. Think about your childhood. Is there evidence that you were the Antichrist? An evil childhood is typically fraught with character-building pain and suffering, such as parents perishing in mysterious fires and close friends accidentally "falling" to the bottom of wells. If you've been evil for as long as you can remember, you probably don't need additional motivation. You're just plain nasty.

An evil childhood is typically fraught with character-building pain and suffering—such as close friends accidentally "falling" down a well.

The Evil Laugh—A Must-Have

There are a number of excellent ways to enhance your evil persona, from feigning a foreign accent to exaggerating a physical defect or tick to cultivating a clannish following among teenagers. However, the most essential skill by far is an evil laugh.

how to do an evil laugh The evil laugh is a defining characteristic of any supervillain, and you will find yourself calling on it quite regularly as you exult in your own wickedness. There are many different laughs to choose from, each signifying varying degrees of derangement.

Dependably evil laughs, in varying degrees of magnitude:

Ha Ha Ha

He-he-he-he-he

Muahahahaha

Bwah-ha-ha-ha-ha!!!

HAHAHAHAHAHAHAHAHAHAHAHAHA

Once you have decided upon a laugh, practice it every day. Take a deep breath, relax, and feel yourself laugh like a crazed hyena. When you have mastered the basic laugh, learn all its different chortles and inflections, exploring the many ways it can inspire fear. Imagine a variety of scenarios when you might employ your laugh.

ha! ha! h

MUAHA

Bwa-ha-

Best Times to Use Your Evil Laugh

- When revealing your master plan
- During a bank heist
- Before dispatching your arch-nemesis to a tank of hungry piranhas
- While standing over the conquered enemy masses
- After your evil scheme has gone off without a hitch
- After instructing your henchmen in some vile deed
- Before unleashing your weapon of mass destruction
- After pressing the enormous red button of doom
- In ironic glee just as the heroes are sneaking up from behind
- While locked inside an insane asylum
- Any time you feel overwhelmed with evil satisfaction

Chapter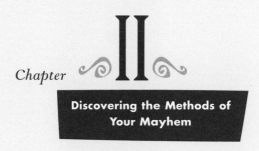

Discovering the Methods of Your Mayhem

"So what are we doing tonight, Brain?"
"The same thing we do every night, Pinky. Try to take over the world!"

— *Pinky and the Brain, future rulers of mankind*

Careers for the Evil-doer

With so many options to choose from, selecting the right evil career can be challenging. The most important thing is to choose a field you enjoy. What excites you? Is it the thrill of intercontinental warfare? The homespun pleasures of blackmail? The peace and solitude of the mad scientist's laboratory?

criminal mastermind Imagine being head of your own illicit empire, complete with legions of thuggish lackeys, heaps of tax-free income, offices in every neighborhood, and connections from police headquarters to city hall—it's every aspiring evil-doer's dream! But how do you land such an enviable position?

Start out small. Multinational evil empires aren't built in a day, and there will be plenty of time to expand your influence later. Find a field of crime that you like, such as bank robbery or intimidation, and practice it. Spend some time making contacts in the underworld and mastering the nuances of your craft. When you're ready, hire a few henchmen and experiment with giving them a signature "look"—a style that makes them stand out from the other henchmen and tells the world who's boss (you). Gradually expand your turf, and be sure to pick up a fluffy white cat to stroke constantly.

As you grow your crime ring, you may encounter resistance from other would-be criminal masterminds. Don't give them a second thought. Who is an evil genius? You are. Don't let some gang of brainless bullies run you out of town, even if they start tossing flaming bricks through your windows. Remember, you can always vaporize the tedious interlopers with your secret death ray. (Note: It is important to put development of the secret death ray on a fast track, just in case.) When the time comes to remove any opposing masterminds, be sure to offer their best henchmen a choice between joining you and jumping into a vat of bubbling acid. You can never have enough resourceful minions at your disposal.

necromancer If graveyards and funeral parlors are your cup of tea, becoming a necromancer may be the right evil career choice for you. Good career entry points include occultists, dabblers in voodoo, grave diggers, morticians, possessed eight-year-old girls, and inheritors of scary books written in cahoots with the Devil.

First, whether by inheritance or other ruse, obtain some sort of Book of Evil. As described in the Tools of the Evil Trade chapter, these blasphemous tomes are excellent sources of bizarre ritual. You can get most sorcerous books from your local occult book-shop, though they've also been known to turn up inside ancient tombs, under lock and key at certain universities, and hidden in the rafters of abandoned Victorian houses.

With your Book of Evil in hand, your next objective is to obtain corpses to people your army of the undead. The local cemetery is probably your best bet, but don't overlook nearby battlefields, the morgue, or simply constructing your own! (Consult your Book of Evil for instructions.)

Once your army is assembled, locate a village of medieval peasants to menace. If none is within easy reach, use whatever happy or prosperous community is nearby. Stake out a deserted mansion to make your base of operations. Once you're set up, send forth your legions of the living dead to attack the townsfolk and transform them into zombies with every bite. Soon you will have an obedient army of the undead, which can then be sent to more towns, and more, until the world is yours.

WARNING: Known side effects of necromancy include loss of hair, pale skin, foul stench, tomb rot, eyes melting from their sockets, mind-boggling insanity, and eternal damnation.

When obtaining corpses to people your army of the undead, the local cemetery is your best bet.

Quick ⌛ Fix!

No time to awaken an army of the undead?
Try these quick alternatives:

- Backup your genuine undead with cardboard reinforcements.

- Paint a large curtain with a trompe l'oeil scene depicting hundreds of thousands of undead eager to do your bidding. Hang it behind you whenever you confront the townsfolk.

- Create holographic undead and project them onto a local church.

- Fashion bodies of the undead out of papier-mâché. Add tissue-paper hair and dress them in rags.

corporate bastard   "Family, religion, friendship. These are the three demons you must slay if you wish to succeed in business." — C. Montgomery Burns, owner, Springfield Nuclear Power Plant

Thanks to the expansion of the global economy, the career of corporate bastard is considered one of the most rewarding among evil-doers today. Generally speaking, there are two ways to become a corporate bastard:

1. Start your own business, building a multinational empire from the ground up.

2. Go to work for an existing multinational empire and claw your way to the top.

If you opt for the first approach, you will probably need a product or service to sell. It does not have to be anything created by you, as intellectual theft is acceptable, encouraged, and really not that difficult. If building your own multinational empire still sounds like too much work, you may want to consider the second route. When pursuing option two, be resourceful. Will seducing a superior with your irresistibly tempting powers land you the job? Go ahead. Can you embezzle funds and use them to bribe key players in senior management? If so, your ascent to the corner office in corporate headquarters will be that much more rapid. Whatever it is that makes you special, don't be afraid to use it to further your career goals. If anyone should discover your methods, eliminate them.

Your total lack of ethics should make climbing the corporate ladder an enjoyably wicked game. Before long you should be in a position of supreme power and able to direct your attention outward. This is the time to crush your competition, no matter how small and seemingly innocuous.

If competition does exist, it must be disposed of, whether by hostile takeover, litigious whimsy, or predatory tactics, such as selling your own product at a tremendous loss in order to drive all others into bankruptcy. You may even choose to make a pact with the dark gods as part of your long-term strategic planning.

Eventually all competition will be obliterated and you can spend your time gloating at the contemptible masses beneath you. This is perhaps one of the most rewarding aspects of being a corporate bastard (other than the money). Enjoy it at every opportunity. And why not? You earned it.

Go to work for an existing multinational empire and claw your way to the top.

To become a first-rate mad scientist, you'll need two important qualities: superior intelligence and mind-boggling insanity.

mad scientist Mad science has never gone out of style among the intellectually gifted and socially awkward. Its practitioners, primarily introverts, are in a unique position to rain down unimaginable terror on the world at large. A key benefit of mad science is the element of surprise. Unlike the corporate bastard whose evil is widely acknowledged in the media, the mad scientist is a loner, often entirely unheard of until he or she unveils a masterwork of hideous evil. The effect can be delightfully shocking.

To become a first-rate mad scientist, you'll need two important qualities: superior intelligence and mind-boggling insanity. The former is important because you'll use it to devise and create your diabolical inventions. While the second, insanity, may not seem necessary now, it is vital to your cause. A healthy perspective will seriously impede your progress as a mad scientist, greatly limiting the scope of what you are capable of achieving.

Your main goal will be to build gigantic and powerful inventions such as weather machines, doomsday devices, and giant robotic spider monsters. Re-creating life is another excellent choice as long as it results in an unstoppable menace. You may also want to attain a laboratory assistant, as they can be quite useful for throwing large switches and seeking out brains for the master. The next step is up to you. Some mad scientists try to rule the world, others to destroy it. Many delve into organized crime, using their inventions to rob Fort Knox or vaporize a favorite city. A few content themselves with unleashing their creations upon mankind. Whatever you choose, you'll feel confident in your role as a superior being who knows what's best for the world. If that means replacing the human race with an army of robotic slaves, so be it.

black knight One of the most gratifying evil careers is that of soldier of darkness. It allows you to ride forth on a jet black steed, murder your enemy in one fell blow, and bring nightmares to every corner of the land. If this sounds good to you, consider the career of black knight.

The first thing to tend to is your appearance. Do not forsake this, as it will inspire unending terror in your enemies as well as numerous death metal album covers. Black knights are normally between six and eight feet tall, dress in black spiked battle armor, and wear huge antlered helmets. They also commonly wield swords or axes in both hands, and skulls or severed heads typically dangle from their waists. Packs of wolves and flocks of ravens, their servants and harbingers of darkness, follow them everywhere.

Black knights are more than carefully wrought images, however. They are death personified. As such, you may need to start out small before realizing your true infernal potential. Many begin as soldiers in an army, working their way up the ranks until they can finally skewer the general on his own blade. Others go for the more solitary route, becoming dark wanderers that travel from town to town, leaving carnage and destruction in their wake.

Once you have gained some power and experience, you will want to devote your time to the main reason you became a black knight: mindless bloodshed. Send forth any armies you have, raining destruction upon neighboring kingdoms. Ultimately, it all comes down to one thing: crush your enemies, see them driven before you, and hear the lamentation of their women. That's all that truly matters, and as long as the rivers are running red with blood, you'll know you've succeeded in a job well done.

One of the most gratifying evil careers is that of soldier of darkness.

horror-movie villain A popular choice due to its high visibility and glamorous reputation, a career as a horror-movie villain is certain to give you a feeling of accomplishment. Done well, a single film can launch a lifelong career with scores of sequels. Even if your films are not hugely successful, you will enjoy stalking scantily clad teenagers through the woods, making phone calls from inside the house, and terrorizing hospital staffs.

Image is paramount to the horror-movie villain. Spend some time developing your screen persona, adding signature props and costume elements to help define your methods and personal style. Some good props include:

- Hockey mask
- Glove with knife-tipped-fingers
- Chainsaw
- Hangman's noose
- Puzzle box
- Incredibly large knife

You will also want to gain immortality, which is a bit more challenging. In the old days, getting hit by lightning would do it every time. These days, you'll need to be more inventive, perhaps experimenting with nuclear waste and radioactive spills. Some of the old methods still seem to work, however, and you may want to consider them:

- Make a pact with the devil
- Get sentenced to the electric chair
- Wear a mystic amulet while you are gunned down in a toy store
- Make a deal with a creepy voodoo woman to avenge the death of your child
- Drown in a river while your camp counselors are too busy having sex to notice, have your mom kill the lovebirds and then, in the sequel, arise from the watery depths

*A career as a horror-movie villain is
certain to give you a feeling of accomplishment.*

There are numerous ways to become a supernatural avatar.

Whichever method you choose, stalk your movie victims with care, allowing them to trip several times and occasionally even to get away. Let your theme music travel with you, as you appear across the lake and behind shaded windows. Finally, make them emit the most bloodcurdling screams possible, as they bury a hatchet in your head and discover that doesn't stop you. It's all in good fun. If they should discover that fire, electricity, or a proper burial is your one weakness, don't worry. Your body will reanimate somehow (it always does), and you will live to slay another day.

avatar for a god/demon/supernatural creature beyond all comprehension Don't want to put in the effort it takes to be an evil overlord but still desire the destruction of all mankind? Maybe you should become a supernatural avatar. An avatar is really just a facilitator. You unleash the evil being and reap the rewards of his or her destructive tendencies. This career is ideal for apprentice sorcerers and those who like meddling in Things Man Was Not Meant to Know.

There are numerous ways to become a supernatural avatar. These include:

1. Find a copy of the *Necronomicon*
2. Open the mummy's tomb
3. Steal the idol from the island natives
4. Wear the ancient mystic amulet
5. Free the supernatural horror from its thousand-year prison

Once you've let the monstrosity take over, there's not much left to do except sit back and watch. And scream in anguish. And claw your eyes out. And feel the flesh rip from your bones as the ancient god is reborn again and grows forty feet tall, devours everything that exists, and brings about the destruction of all humanity.

marketing executive   Less overtly evil than other evil career options, the marketing executive is nonetheless an insidious purveyor of nongood. From spam to subliminal advertising, this evil-doer creeps like a fog, slipping into the citizenry's subconscious with a thousand mind-melding messages. In the words of Keyser Soze, "The greatest trick the devil ever pulled was convincing the world he didn't exist," and the marketing executive exploits this ruse to the fullest.

For decades, marketing executives have been promoting the idea that advertising and sponsorship are simply healthy extensions of capitalism with no serious effect on people's behavior. The result is complete freedom of evil expression. No matter how malicious your intent, as an evil marketing executive you have the power to promulgate your ideas willy-nilly, winning unwitting converts to your cause around the globe.

The marketing executive is an insidious purveyor of nongood.

Evil Marketing Executive To-Do List:

- Buy an avant-garde suit and unusual eyeglasses
- Devise evil campaign messaging with a simple call to action, such as "Send cash now!"
- Purchase prime placement in broadcast and print media
- Coerce endorsements from dull-witted celebrities
- Incorporate in the Bahamas, open a bank account, and prepare for arrival of cash

World domination is one of the most rewarding evil objectives.

Objectives and Goals

An evil-doer without an objective is a sorry sight, slumped on the couch, death ray half-finished and abandoned, dull gaze directed at the television, orange residue of cheese puffs staining the lips and tongue. Don't let your sinister potential go to waste! Identify an evil purpose now and get your dark energies on track for success. The three most common evil goals are outlined below, but feel free to follow your heart. If your dark deed isn't listed here, that doesn't mean it's not evil. In fact, it might be the worst thing anybody's ever done!

1. World Domination

This is the biggie. World domination is one of the most powerful and rewarding of all evil objectives. Surprisingly, it's not as easy as one might think. It actually takes a lot of work. Here are a few of the sinister possibilities.

economic The brute force inherent in a multinational corporation makes it an excellent means of perpetrating global evil. Economic oppression is, in many ways, superior to the old-school approach of mass warfare, if only because it is faster and has a higher profit margin (no need to produce costly weapons). What you will need to do is make the global market dependent on you for the products you make and the jobs you provide, and then eliminate the competition until you become a total monopoly. Hotels on Park Place and Boardwalk are also a good idea. Should you play your cards right, your corporation will gain supreme power and your lobbyists will eventually have more say than the political leaders themselves. Each decision you make will influence millions of lives, and the prosperity of the world will depend on your benevolence. Provided you have any, that is.

military This is the classic form of world domination in which you take over Earth through sheer military might. To achieve this end, you will want to begin building your destructive arsenal as soon as possible, including but certainly not limited to armies, death rays, doomsday devices, and giant robotic spider monsters. You'll also want to formulate your master plan, train your troops in the subtle arts of looting and pillaging, and form strategic alliances (you can break them later if necessary). When you feel you are ready, unleash your dogs of war on an unsuspecting world. Send forth destruction like Earth has never seen, and take over the planet in one fell swoop. The old methods are often the best and, in this case, the most satisfying.

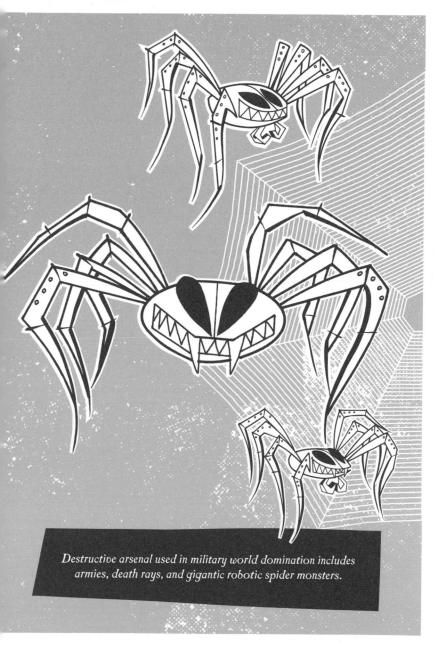

Destructive arsenal used in military world domination includes armies, death rays, and gigantic robotic spider monsters.

shadow government The use of shadow governments and secret societies is another viable means of world domination. In a shadow government, you enjoy anonymity while exercising complete control over those "in charge." The actual government does not even need to know you are there! To implement a shadow government, train a few dozen reliable spies and place them in pivotal positions throughout the infrastructure of the country you wish to control, including powerful roles in the military, Freemasons, NRA, and the post office. If you are tripped up by any actual authority figures, dispatch them and replace them with identical clones or animatronics. Conspiracy theorists may strike close to home on occasion, but they are not a significant threat since no one ever believes them.

The use of shadow governments and secret societies is another viable means of world domination.

ideological   Belief systems can be easily manipulated to suit your needs. For example, you might become the spokesperson for an ideology so ludicrous it sweeps the planet like a bad haircut. If you know such a philosophy, set yourself up as its head now. If not, create your own. Your ideology can be religious, political, or even personal. The key is to make it irresistible by promising outlandish benefits to believers. However, be careful to make this payoff contingent upon some far-off event, ideally something either extremely unlikely or impossible to verify. Never promise outlandish payoffs immediately, or your ideology will fail faster than you can say flapjacks. Instead, assure believers that they will enjoy untold tax-free riches, immortality, or eternal happiness after the revolution and their painful deaths. To make your ideology extra compelling, devise a horrible punishment for nonbelievers.

mass media   This is a fairly new form of world domination, one that has proven to be remarkably effective over the last several decades. Rather than using military might or multinational corporations to take over the world, you can instead employ the insidious power of media and language. To achieve this end, you will want to control every type of information the people receive, and then set up the world in a "bubble" reality. You see, if the public doesn't know that a particular war is going on, that we don't really need oil for cars, or that the president is a brain-sucking alien from Dimension X, then no one can get angry about it. Furthermore, if you promote specific world views in the media people watch or read, then the public can be manipulated into a mindset of your choosing. People will think they are free, but in reality, they are slaves, mindless and controlled by the very entertainment they pay to see—world domination for the new millennium.

People will think they are free, but in reality, they are slaves.

Ten Great Things about the End of the World

1. Plenty of free parking

2. No more boy bands

3. Radiation grants cool mutant powers

4. Boiling seas like hot tubs

5. Whore of Babylon is a total babe

6. Get to watch the moon turn to blood

7. Ravaging demons make commute more interesting

8. Bio-plagues turn people funny colors

9. Four Horsemen of the Apocalypse—party animals!

10. Heart-to-heart talks with C'thulhu before he eats you

2. Global Destruction

For as long as man has walked the earth he has longed to destroy it. At last, you can be the one that makes it happen!

biblical apocalypse While many evil masterminds eschew religion, the biblical Armageddon is still popular among the hopeful. This classically depicted apocalypse is quite sinister, featuring a collapsing sky, the dead rising from their graves, and cities crumbling to dust. You might wonder about the common allegation that in the end good will triumph over evil, but that probably won't happen. The real problem with destroying the world by biblical apocalypse is timing. How long will you have to wait for the seas to spew fire? Too long, based on experience. If you've got your mind set on cosmic cataclysm, you'll probably have to do it yourself, or at least get it started. See the earlier section on becoming an avatar for more details.

asteroids from space One rogue asteroid could rocket the planet back to the Ice Age. Death from above is thus another nefarious means of world destruction. Unfortunately it is rather difficult to cause such collisions intentionally. You will need two things to bring about heavenly mayhem: a good-sized asteroid and some sort of tractor beam. The first is easy enough, as they're practically everywhere. You can even use the moon if you're so inclined. The second is a bit more difficult, requiring as it does a powerful gravity generator. Although this may seem like a tall order, don't despair. If you don't have the greatest evil minds ever born working for you, recruit them immediately and inform them of the task at hand. Develop a backup plan just in case.

*You will need two things: a good-sized asteroid
and some sort of tractor beam.*

As a high-ranking politician, you'll enjoy the freedom to indulge your every evil impulse.

3. Widespread Misery

Even to many would-be evil-doers, destroying the world is scary. If it is gone, who will you torment? And yet, controlling the world doesn't quite appeal either. It sounds like too much work! If that's how you feel, disseminating misery and grief may be your raison d'être. It's not about oblivion and it's not about being in charge. It's about pain and lots of it.

the great old ones So long as you don't have any particular destruction in mind, but simply devastation in general, unleashing powerful supernatural forces could be an effective strategy. This option is especially interesting due to the myriad horrors you can summon forth, ranging from Christian devils to Babylonian gods to unpronounceable Enochian demons. Be sure to study the work of H. P. Lovecraft for details on these obscure and unsavory beings from times long past. Certain ones are so mind-boggling that their mere manifestation can cause mass insanity. You'll find complete recipes for calling up all manner of vile demon in the *Necronomicon,* which, unfortunately, has been lost for centuries. Listen, if being evil was easy everyone would do it.

politics Perhaps the best way to promote universal suffering is through politics. As a high-ranking politician, you'll enjoy the freedom to indulge your every evil impulse. Rather than go through the arduous task of building up your own army of thugs, you can use your nation's existing military forces to do your bidding. Best of all, most top political positions come with an evil lair all set up and ready for occupancy. Crowds will gather to hear you pronounce your evil dictates. Even the political vehicle of choice, the black limousine, suits your dark persona perfectly.

criminal activities Consider taking part in a wide variety of criminal activities. These are the lifeblood of the supervillain, the source of your evil income and personal entertainment. While crimes make you smile, they'll make everyone else frown. You may worry that you're only one person, that you can spread only so much misery through a few ill deeds here and there. Don't think about it that way. Being evil isn't always about achieving your goal. Sometimes it just means staying on track, practicing your craft, and making progress day by day. Remember to enjoy the journey.

police state Certainly one of the most miserable conditions available, the police state is guaranteed to ensure that everyone you know is filled with despair. Start by taking control of the national government. Install as much automated surveillance equipment as you can afford. If you can't swing enough cash for actual cameras, spray paint old shoe boxes and milk cartons black and tape them to the ceiling, angling them to focus on workers' desks, on the entrance to the supermarket, on the houses in which people live, and on any other suitable spot. Dress in a nauseating shade of gray and encourage—or even force—others to do the same. Post signs threatening horrible punishments for undefined acts. Pass laws insisting drapes be drawn at all times and that conversations be spoken in flat, monotone free of any emotion. Outlaw color, song, and dance. Make mime performances mandatory. If things get dull, accuse a colleague of doublespeak but refuse to explain what that means.

soul accumulation   Many evil-doers enjoy the sport of soul accumulation. Originally the exclusive purview of the Devil, soul capture is now widely practiced by ordinary evil people thanks to widespread access to the black arts. The most common technique of acquisition is the soul contract, in which you are awarded ownership of the soul in exchange for granting the donor's desire. Through the black arts, it is also possible to steal souls and to defraud unsuspecting victims of their souls. Though souls do not have any real market value, they are fun to collect and a true symbol of your evil status.

Chapter

III

Thwarting the Forces of Good

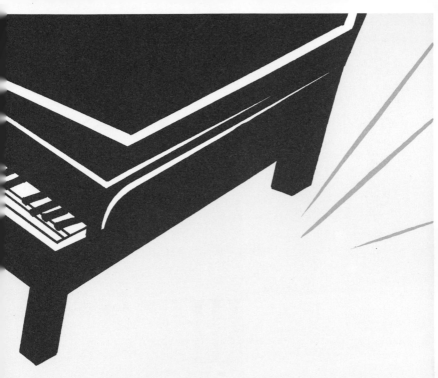

"Superman has morals. He has ethics, he is unrelentingly good. Because of that, I will win."

—*Lex Luthor*

Now that you've begun an evil career, you need to understand that there are individuals who will to try to stop your nefarious deeds. Known as the forces of good, they will arrive time and time again just when you're ready to unleash your robotic army on an unsuspecting continent.

So just who are these guys? Why do they do the things they do? What could they possibly find wrong with ravaging the earth and inflicting humanity with forty years of darkness? To gain a better understanding of how the opposition thinks, review the following three scenarios.

Scenario #1 You are walking through a city park when you suddenly come upon a young child skipping along, lollipop in hand, singing a merry song. What do you do?

As a member of the forces of good, you *don't* steal the candy. That's right, instead of ripping the lollipop from that little pudgy hand and luxuriating in the inevitable tears, you pat the child on the head and watch protectively as he or she continues down the path.

You suddenly come upon a young child skipping along, lollipop in hand. What do you do?

Scenario #2 A bank robbery is taking place. Masked men are carrying out sacks of money when suddenly they are forced to stop in their tracks. Some guy in spandex and a cape has appeared and is shouting "Be gone evil-doers!" Which of these people is you?

As a member of the forces of good, you would be the guy in the cape..That's right, the cape. Not the bank robbers or the criminal mastermind behind them, but the fellow in the tights.

Scenario #3 You have come upon members of an evil cult performing an ancient ritual of magic and sorcery. They are reading from an occult tome and as they chant strange words, a horde of supernatural demons arise to destroy the world. What do you do?

As a member of the forces of good you actually try to *stop* the ritual. You don't want to help these supernatural beings promote wanton destruction. Instead, you rush in, disrupt the spell, blow out the candles, and give everyone present a good talking-to about fire danger.

As a member of the forces of good, you would be the guy in the cape. That's right, the cape.

The Good Mentality

Many different qualities make up the good mentality. They vary from person to person, and some are often stronger than others, but in general a member of the forces of good will have at least one of the following character traits. A rare menace of a hero will possess all six.

Conscience (con · shintz) The most common trait among heroes is what's called a conscience. Because of it, they will obey the law, keep their word, and not even consider enslaving all humanity. Moreover, they will strive to protect the innocent and serve the common good whenever possible, a fact that can be exploited to your benefit. For example, should an unplanned confrontation between you and a hero occur, force the cape-wearing do-gooder to choose between bringing you to justice and saving the city from your doomsday device. They will choose the city every time.

Compassion (cum · pa · shun) Compassion is another typical characteristic of the classic do-gooder. Otherwise known as the selfless desire to help others, this is what makes them care for puppies and help old ladies across the street. Do not even try to comprehend this behavior, and be forewarned that compassionate people also tend to be the most annoying. Expect a lot of "Why do you have to be so bad?" and "People like you make Baby Jesus cry." Resist such entreaties all you can, as well as their constant attempts to show you the true meaning of Christmas.

Pity (pit · ee) Pity is perhaps a hero's greatest weakness. The unthinkable will happen and your evil scheme will have gone all wrong. You will be blubbering for mercy, knowing that nothing can save you. Then the hero will stop. Rather than killing you to wipe out the obvious threat you are, the hero will strike a dignified pose and say, "No. I'm not going to kill you. I'm not like you, evil guy!" Instead, the authorities will come to take you away. That's a relief, of course, because you can always escape their clutches.

Honesty (ahn · es · tee) Heroes always tell the truth no matter what the consequences. This can be useful when it comes to isolating them from their support network, be it superhero friends, sidekicks, or life-saving pets. First, entice your hero by coercion or trickery into a situation or act, ideally involving one of the cardinal sins, that will disappoint the support network. Then, leak the indiscretion to the news media and his close family. The hero by his own nature will be forced to confess, and he will soon find himself abandoned by friends, loved ones, and even his sidekick.

Courage (coor · adj) Heroes have been known to take a bullet for the president, leap into burning buildings, and try to defuse the bomb instead of running for their lives. Why they're not wiped out already we'll never know. They also won't necessarily back down in the face of overwhelming odds, instead standing tall as your minions surround them with pointy weapons. Bravery must always be taken into account when dealing with heroes. Just when you think you've got them beat, they'll suddenly pounce on you shouting, "Not today, Fritz!"

Honor (ah · ner) Members of the forces of good tend to abide by an abstraction called honor. This is a personal code of rules that they base their lives around and follow to the death if need be. Some evil people possess codes of honor as well, though you must do all you can not to fall into this trap. Consider the following example: "You did well, MacGyver! You managed to escape my maze of death! I won't kill you . . . this time." What the hell is that? Kill him for God's sake! He's only going to come back next episode and thwart your evil scheme!

Hero Types (and How to Thwart Them)

Your virtuous foes will be easy to recognize because, like evil-doers, they tend to emulate one of a handful of archetypes. Luckily, each has a weakness. If you should ever find yourself in a pickle, facing certain incarceration (or worse) at the hands of a white knight do-gooder, be vigilant and watch for the glimmer of opportunity, remembering the soft spots identified below.

defender of justice The most common hero type is the defender of justice. These are the crime fighters and caped crusaders who uphold the law and try to stop evil in all its forms. Unfortunately, these misguided champions are guaranteed to be a major thorn in your side, thwarting your schemes at every turn, popping up when you least expect them, escaping your best death traps, threatening to send you up the river, and ransacking your lair in all-out brawls with your henchmen. They also like to form entire leagues of heroes, which means you might have to fight a whole team of these spandex-wearing maniacs.

how to thwart them The defenders of justice are perhaps your greatest enemy, so it will behoove you to actively pursue their capture and demise. If you should happen to snare one, for evil god's sake dispatch them quickly. Even if you long to use your excruciatingly slow hourglass death device, resist the urge. Heroes typically escape this kind of situation.

You might have to fight a whole team of these spandex-wearing maniacs.

This gritty antihero spells nothing but trouble.

angry cool guy Another hero that pops up everywhere these days is the angry cool guy. This gritty antihero spells nothing but trouble and can usually be identified by his leather jacket, thick scar, and three-day growth of beard. Generally known for their antisocial behavior, these cool characters often get into fistfights and barroom brawls for no good reason. Unfortunately, they also tend to do the right thing in the end, despite their contempt for the rules and their "rebel without a cause" attitude. Don't bother trying to convert them, as nothing brings them more pleasure than giving a villain his due.

how to thwart them Your best bet with the angry cool guy is to look even more gritty and hardcore than he does. Perhaps you are soul mates, he may wonder. Perhaps you too suffered some early loss and isolation that turned you into an angry cool guy and defender of the weak. If you are in luck, he will stride back into the sunset and leave you in evil peace.

vixen Tempting, saucy, and often clad in a ridiculously skimpy costume, the vixen is a serious threat. Above all, avoid close personal contact with these hero types, as they have been known to use their stimulating powers to ensnare many an evil supervillain. Renowned for their low necklines and razor-sharp wit, they aren't afraid to speak their minds and will often put the more macho heroes in their places. This is their only good quality, however, because they otherwise feel a tremendous need to kick evil ass all over the place. They will smash your crime syndicate and foil your sinister schemes, all without breaking a nail.

how to thwart them If possible, throw the vixen into the path of the angry cool guy or vice versa. There is typically a great deal of sexual tension between these two, and distracting them with each other will give you the time you need to organize your ambush.

silent loner   Many an evil-doer has fallen prey to the silent loner. You may be sitting around your lair, minding your own business and plotting nefarious deeds, when suddenly some mysterious stranger rolls into town and starts destroying all you have worked to create. He or she may come in the form of a lone gunslinger, mystical swordsman, or one-man-army out for revenge. Whatever the case, silent loners are nearly unstoppable and will oppose you at every turn. On the plus side, they always travel by themselves, so at least you'll only have one opponent.

how to thwart them   Silent loners by definition have no friends and thus no one to vouch for them, making them ideal candidates for a classic frame-up. Lure them to the scene of the crime, plant a bit of evidence, notify the authorities, and watch the fun. No one really knows Racer X, so how can anyone be certain it wasn't him who burned down city hall?

the sidekick   Beware of sidekicks in all forms, for they are not the harmless idiots you think them to be. These individuals are a real threat and should be taken out at all costs. Why? Because they provide assistance to the hero just when he or she needs it most. The help might come in the form of a distraction, vital clue, or morale-boosting one-liner. Occasionally they can even pull off a genuine rescue, saving the hero from an otherwise terrible death. Be constantly vigilant about their interfering presence, no matter how diminutive.

how to thwart them   Their coordinated outfits make sidekicks fairly easy to spot. Youthful, energetic, and highly annoying, they delight in such phrases as "Jumping Jillipers!" or "Golly Gadzooks!" To eliminate them, first isolate them from the überhero. Being inexperienced, they will often fall for a simple ruse, such as leaving behind an obvious clue that leads them straight to your lair, where their demise awaits.

Silent loners are nearly unstoppable and will oppose you at every turn.

woman warrior The woman warrior who hunts you may be an Amazon through birth, the daughter of a god, or some sort of mythic figure, but whatever her background, she will be well-versed in the battle arts. She will probably wield a sword or bow, though some practitioners prefer enchanted lassos. The woman warrior also tends to dress in armor that protects an amazingly small amount of her body from attack, but don't let the scanty outfit fool you. The abbreviated attire may be her only weakness. This woman means evil-butt-kicking business. Hard to catch due to her proclivity for jumping and flipping about, the woman warrior is truly a force to be reckoned with.

Don't let the scanty outfit fool you. This woman means evil-butt-kicking business.

how to thwart them Women warriors can be extremely dangerous, so it's best to send in the goons for this one and watch from
afar. If your goons fail, attempt—cautiously—to seduce the warrior with your bedeviling charms. This probably won't work, but
the tiny hope that it might makes the effort worth the risk.

swashbuckler   You may think you are safe from the swashbuckler by now, but rare sightings still occur. There are still a number of heroes out there who like swinging from chandeliers while clenching a dagger between their teeth. Also known for their fabulous swordplay, the swashbuckler is as skilled in the arts of romance as he is in heroism. Master of the dance as well as the bedside, his very appearance can cause women to faint and hearts to swoon. If you think the swashbuckler is an unworthy adversary, consider how much he has accomplished while wearing a poofy shirt and breeches. What if you had to wear a poofy shirt and breeches? The world just might be safe from serious evil.

how to thwart them   The swashbuckler is a true swordsman and will fight like a hundred men. Send in a hundred and one.

wise mentor If you're a serious threat to the world, chances are you have spent plenty of time honing some kind of exceptional ability, whether mental, physical, or spiritual. If you did, you probably had a mentor, maybe even a benevolent mentor. Although generally not your main rival, this man or woman can be a tiresome speed bump on the road to evil. The pesky man will send your nemesis on his or her fateful journey after full instruction in the arcane knowledge and martial arts moves necessary to stop you. When it's time to terminate any mentor's shenanigans, look for this thorn-in-your-side on a mountaintop or desert planet, wearing brown robes and uttering cryptic haiku.

how to thwart them Certainly you know all their tricks, but mentors have experience on their side. Still, these troublesome rivals are actually pretty easy to stop. All you need do is challenge them to a duel and then strike them down with your superior skill. Using their last breath, they may point out that destroying them only makes them stronger, but it's never been proven and is probably a bluff.

unlikely hero One of the more obnoxious hero types to emerge over the last several years is the wow-you'd-never-expect-them-to-be-a-hero hero. They manifest themselves as anything from a priest turned detective to a gawky teenager sucked into the D&D universe to a hooker with a heart of gold. Worse, they often travel in packs, especially if age fourteen and a group of social misfits at Camp Wannacannitcha. Please understand it is vitally important that you do *not* dismiss their side-splitting antics as harmless. Why? Because more often than not some chubby kid with glasses will save the day, and you would have gotten away with it, too, if it weren't for those meddling kids.

how to thwart them   Break with the clichés. Try not to be a stereotypical villain. Don't gloat, don't reveal your evil schemes, and don't wear a rubber mask they can yank off to prove it was old man Munson all along! (Zoinks!)

More often than not some chubby kid with glasses will save the day.

Lovable animal companions have the disturbing habit of assisting their masters.

lovable animal companion Your nemeses need not take a humanoid form at all. Dangerous good intentions proliferate in the animal companions that heroes of every ilk are bound to attract. Be it a loyal dog, falcon on the shoulder, or some sort of cutesy ferret, these little bastards are heinous and spell nothing but trouble. Like sidekicks, lovable animal companions have the disturbing habit of assisting their masters. Imagine you have locked up the hero in your dungeon with no possibility of escape, when all of a sudden some damn monkey appears and squeezes through the prison bars with the keys. Or, again imagining the hero in prison, the next thing you know, a seemingly innocuous ferret comes sniffing around at night, discovers the hero, wiggles through your clutches, and runs for help. No cause for alarm, you say to yourself, this unobtrusive creature cannot even talk! But you forget that this loyal companion is masterful at emoting and gesturing. Soon the ground shakes with the approach of avenging hooves. The lesson? Stop that ferret.

how to thwart them Handle any lovable animal companion with the same ruthless guile you would use on any other foe. Just because they are little and adorable does not mean they can weasel out of a duel to the death.

D Death Traps

eath traps are perfect for many situations, especially when death is the objective. You will probably want to come up with your own signature equipment, but until you do, here are a few of the classic models for inspiration.

hall of mirrors Look for this creepy favorite in any fun house or amusement park. An excellent place for final confrontations with heroes, the hall of mirrors wins high marks for ease of use. All you have to do is lure your victims inside by dashing in yourself, and then cackle with glee as they find you reflected back not once but a thousand times. If they try to attack, they will find you are only an illusion, and no matter how hard they look, they will be unable to locate the real you. When you've had enough fun, seal the exits and fill the cramped space with some kind of liquid. Plain water works as well as anything, but why not add food dye for color. Or, for a touch of whimsy, use a sickeningly sweet fruit punch.

The hall of mirrors wins high marks for ease of use.

maze of death Tracing its history back to the Greek legend of King Minos and his dreaded maze-dwelling Minotaur, a gigantic labyrinth of death promises a dramatic end for your most hated heroes. These wonderful mazes are filled with so many twists and turns that escape is near impossible. Behind each corridor terrible death can await through whirling blades or stone statues come to life. You can even place an authentic Minotaur in the middle, poised to devour anyone who crosses its path. (Note: To create a Minotaur, combine a demigod with a bull and wait fifteen to twenty years for the creature to mature to full strength.) To persuade the hero to enter your maze of death, capture the beloved sidekick or animal companion and deposit said loved one in the center of the labyrinth. You'll want to check back later to be sure both the loved one and the hero have safely blundered into a terrible demise.

pit of doom These structures are so ideal for eliminating heroes, they are practically a requirement for any evil lair, no matter how informal. By concealing your pit beneath a trapdoor or bundle of sticks, you can send do-gooders plummeting with nothing more than a false step. For obvious reasons, the top of the line is the bottomless pit (no cleanup), but any pit of doom will work as long as it is deep, inescapable, and placed near an area where you plan to battle heroes. Spend some time practicing your footwork around the pit, so you will be ready when it's time for the final death match. Plenty of henchmen have been known to tumble into these pits by accident, representing a sizable insurance liability. To help limit your risk, it's a good idea to create a Pit of Doom safety video and require your henchmen to view it every six months. As an additional precaution, insist each of them signs a waiver and accepts the risks inherent in being an evil henchman.

Pits of doom are practically a requirement for any evil lair, no matter how informal.

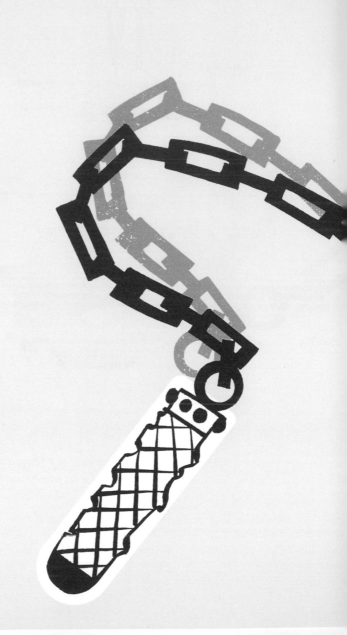

Chapter IV

Tools of the Evil Trade

"Pathetic Earthlings! Hurling your bodies out into the void without the slightest inkling of who or what is out here. If you knew anything about the true nature of the universe, anything at all, you would have hidden from it in terror."

— *Ming the Merciless*, Flash Gordon

Locations for Your Lair

Every evil mastermind needs a base of operations in order to stay organized. Choose your lair carefully, because you'll be spending a lot of time there laughing maniacally, plotting nefarious deeds, and possibly waiting out decades of plague and destruction. If you have any enemies, they will probably show up on your doorstep eventually, so you'll want it to be an impressive edifice to your grandeur. Here are a few worthy lair options to consider.

medieval castle Since the Middle Ages, medieval castles have been among the most popular lairs for evil-doers. They have atmosphere, they're desolate, and they inspire terror in peasants and townsfolk everywhere. Stock your castle with all the basic amenities, including a portcullis, a moat, boiling oil, and a roofline of gargoyles come to life. Many castles also come with an armory for outfitting your minions and a torture chamber for housing unwanted visitors. If you are an evil-doer who likes lounging upon a throne from which you condemn innocent souls to a terrible fate, taking up residence in a dark and gloomy castle is a smart pick.

corporate tower The corporate skyscraper is another excellent base of operations, and one that is being seen with increased frequency these days. It affords you a central location as well as an air of legitimacy, all the while sheltering your profligate scheming. You may also enjoy the sensation of hundreds and perhaps thousands of workers honeycombed in the many floors beneath you, where they pass endless days in thrall to your superiority. Be sure to select a very tall and imposing corporate tower. If a taller tower is constructed nearby, demolish it. If it cannot be safely destroyed without harming your own skyscraper, top your tower with a massive spire crowned with a sharp spike reaching high enough to surpass the apex of your neighbor.

Medieval Castles: They have atmosphere, they're desolate, and they inspire terror in peasants and townsfolk everywhere.

To the untrained eye it looks like nothing more than an isolated shack in the middle of nowhere.

underground secret headquarters of doom Perhaps what you're looking for is a gigantic underground complex housed miles beneath the earth's crust. To the untrained eye the secret entrance looks like nothing more than an isolated shack in the middle of nowhere. But should you take the secret elevator hidden within, all is horribly revealed. Filled with doomsday devices and liberally enhanced with enormous metal doors that slam shut with a nerve-jangling severity, an underground headquarters is a diabolical lair of which you can be proud. The sprawling expanse should provide ample room for the creation of your robot army, and the cryogenic tubes, should you opt to install them, are useful for freezing yourself so that you might awaken at a more auspicious time. Popular for their low energy bills, privacy, and "only a madman could live here" ambience, a subterranean lair is an excellent choice indeed.

hell Hell has long been the favored choice for supernatural creatures and sorcerous evil-doers and should serve nicely as your new home. You will be pleased to find numerous amenities, including demons available to assist you with your evil deeds and countless souls to torment and devour should the days get dull. The Gates of Hell are an excellent defense against angelic attack, and sporting opportunities on the River Styx are within walking distance. The key drawback of Hell is the flesh-scorching climate, although it has the virtue of keeping property values extremely affordable.

You will be pleased to find numerous amenities in Hell, including demons available to assist you with your evil deeds.

fake mountain   The fake mountain with a hollow interior is another appealing site. While on the outside it looks like any other mountain, with the flip of a switch you can transform it into a deadly fortress of doom! Where once stood rock can now stand rocket turrets, as the front opens up to reveal missile launchers and artillery cannons. The central base can easily house your armies of destruction, and the whole thing folds up quite nicely when you are done playing with it. The only caveat with the fake mountain is that you should not place it in the middle of a city. For some reason, they are too often noticed there.

airship   For the evil-doer on the go, the airship can serve as an especially mobile base of operations. Some may worry that an airship will be cramped and uncomfortable, but that doesn't need to be the case. Plenty of airships are so large, entire generations of henchmen are born and raised not knowing they are even on a transport. Depending on your needs, you may want to build a state-of-the-art intergalactic vessel. If budget constraints are a factor, consider refurbishing a used zeppelin, private jet, or hot-air balloon. If you happen to have a science-defying lightning gun, you'll enjoy using it to rain down terror from above as you glide through the stratosphere unharmed.

space station   Some of the very best evil-lair real estate isn't even located on Earth. That's right, a space station may be right for you, superb for plotting out your evil deeds far out of reach of any underfunded do-gooder. Nowadays space fortresses are standard issue with former Star Wars and SDI technology and can be easily retrofitted with disrupter rays and cloaking fields. They make an excellent base of operations for bringing about the destruction of the earth, particularly if self-preservation is a priority. You may suffer from occasional alien attacks and the periodic asteroid, but the space station is a first-rate lair and should not be overlooked.

amusement park   Although considered gimmicky for years, the amusement park lair has seen a resurgence in popularity in recent times. The reason is simple: There's just no denying the evil current coursing just below the surface of all those squeals of joy. The décor can easily be transformed into a carnival of horrors, with the roller coasters becoming death machines, the fun houses laced with booby traps, and a hall of mirrors at the end for confronting the heroes. You can also establish themed areas throughout your park, such as Apocalypse Land, Evil Clown Land, or even Nightmares Made Flesh Land. The tunnel of love also offers endless possibilities for becoming the tunnel of screams. If you have children, this lair will mean hours of endless fun for the whole family.

The amusement park lair has seen a resurgence in popularity.

haunted woods Many evil-doers want nothing more than to live in an ancient forest filled with wolves and demons. The foreboding trees and unearthly fog are excellent for creating a spooky atmosphere, and the ghosts who haunt such places hold the promise of providing plenty of decorative screams and moans. Branches of trees will seem to tear at the hair and clothes of all who trespass, rendering them gelatinous with fright. You may even find that the other inhabitants of your deep, dark woods—wicked witch in the candy house, insane hermit in rundown cabin, evil sorceress in glass-castle hallucination—may stimulate your creativity.

dungeon Perfect for warlords and wizards, a roomy dungeon is a superb spot from which to plot the destruction of nearby kingdoms. Fill your catacombs with the undead, monsters, and supernatural beasts, with an orc sitting on a chest of gold behind every turn. You can also hide death traps throughout the corridors, each one more deadly and extravagant than the last. The only problem with dungeon lairs is a scarce supply of adventurers intruding to explore them. When they do show up, be prepared for their tiresome antics, as well as the constant sound of dice rolling in the background.

abandoned church Another excellent lair possibility is an abandoned church, preferably in a section of the city no one ever goes to anymore. Besides the irony of such a locale, these former holy grounds are aesthetically ideal for creating a sinister atmosphere. Dark, atmospheric and filled with otherworldly forces, they're tailor-made for evil geniuses. Adorn the entrance with an upside-down crucifix for emphasis. Inside, construct blasphemous altars and secret chambers filled with insane cultists chanting rites to unspeakable gods. If heresy and sacrilege make you smile, and you're planning to fill your calendar with satanic rituals, an abandoned church might just be the lair for you.

Many evil-doers want nothing more than to live in an ancient forest filled with wolves and demons.

Evil-doers who are also supernatural monstrosities might want to consider settling down in an ancient tomb.

ancient tomb Evil-doers who are also supernatural monstrosities might want to consider settling down in an ancient tomb. This choice is especially popular among vampires and mummies, although any form of pure evil should find that an ancient tomb makes an easily converted live-work space. The stone halls and Gothic décor will make you the envy of every angst-ridden teenager, and a coffin or mausoleum is usually available for your personal convenience. You can sleep until the foolish adventurers rouse you from your thousand-year slumber, and then devour not just them but all mankind.

desert island Perfect for the evil-doer in need of a vacation, the desert island is a wonderful place to set up shop. The scenic locale is ideal for relieving stress, while providing an earthly paradise to destroy and despoil. Island natives are usually provided at no extra cost, thus giving you a people to torment, enslave, and rule over like a god. Desert islands are also well suited to the creation of mutant races, so mad scientists take note. If you've had it up to here with the hustle and bustle of city life and are dreaming of something new, then you may want to consider this exotic alternative.

If none of these suggestions appeal, you might consider haunting a public venue such as a theater, stadium, or bridge. As you explore your lair options, remember that you don't have to settle for less than your ideal. If you don't find what you're looking for right away, rent an abandoned Victorian house on a weed-covered lot and take your time searching for the perfect evil place.

Evil Henchmen Guide

Unfortunately, most evil-doers cannot accomplish their schemes on their own. There is simply too much to do and too many people to terrorize. To stay on top of your evil plan, you will need to recruit henchmen or mindless slaves to carry out menial tasks. There are as many kinds of evil henchmen as there are evil overlords. Which kind is right for you?

classic thugs The classic thug has been the favored henchman of criminal masterminds for decades. Be they mobsters with itchy trigger fingers or gangs of unwashed ruffians, nothing inspires fear quite like hired thugs. Slow on the uptake, their dull wit will generally see them through simple tasks plainly articulated, such as "Bring me the money" or "Kill them." A nostalgic choice, thugs evoke simpler days when all you needed to set up evil shop was a waterfront hideout and a good cigar. They're also a dime a dozen, so they're an economical choice even if you burn through them like kindling.

mutant race These unholy abominations are perfect for the evil genius who likes messing with God's creation. Using genetic realignment, create an army of cat people, fish people, alligator people, or even walking tree people, as your needs require. Particularly suited to living on desert islands, these hybrids possess the best of both worlds and tend to be faster, stronger, and just plain better than any human troops could ever hope to be. Be forewarned, however, that they can be rebellious. Manage them with tough love and you should avoid most uprisings. To be extra safe, include a doomsday gene that enables you to wipe them out with the push of a button.

Create an army of cat people, fish people, alligator people, or even walking tree people, as your needs require.

robot warriors If you are looking for an unstoppable army of killing machines unhampered by such weaknesses as mercy and compassion, robot warriors are for you. These metallic automatons will serve you without question, destroying your foes with their ray guns. They also are remarkably resilient, able to take an amazing amount of damage before finally being blown to pieces. A variety of forms are usually available, such as humanoid, tank-shaped, and fifty-story-high monstrosities beyond all comprehension. The only real problem with robot warriors is that they have an unfortunate tendency to rise up and destroy their human masters. Thankfully, most lack the capacity for original thought and can be sufficiently fooled by a silver jumpsuit and digitally altered voice.

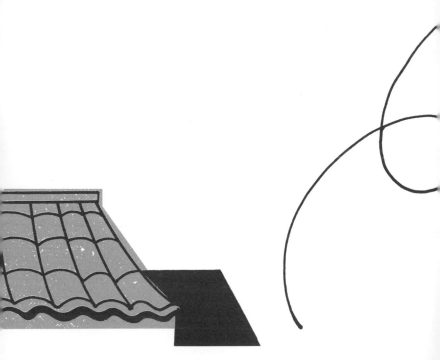

Ninjas have style, dash, and more than a little skill in the fighting arts.

ninjas A favorite for good reason, ninjas have style, dash, and more than a little skill in the fighting arts. These masters of assassination will bring death on silent wings, eliminating your enemies and defending your base with ease. They can also be used for spying purposes, with most of them able to become invisible and to scramble up walls like a spider. A true force to be reckoned with, it's no wonder ninjas have won "Henchmen of the Year" more often than any of their rivals.

Evil-doers might want to consider alien invaders as their henchmen of choice.

alien life forms Evil-doers willing to sell out all humanity might want to consider alien invaders as their henchmen of choice. These off-world entities will rarely hesitate to devour your enemies with relish. They can usually be found in a wide variety of forms, including big-headed "grays," parasitic face-huggers, and giant slobbering mounds of teeth and claws. These extraplanetary minions are also ideal for abducting your enemies, and will gladly probe them in the most uncomfortable places. Should you desire allies with a higher intelligence, or just want something with acid for blood, alien life forms should serve you nicely.

demented clowns Children have long known the truth: Clowns are evil. As such, they can make excellent henchmen for all your nightmarish needs. Perfect for terrifying young and old alike, these monstrous fiends relish in hiding under beds and hanging around carnivals after closing time. Being insane, they are capable of performing the vilest acts, including those that make more traditional henchmen balk. With their enormous floppy shoes, deranged laughter, and greasepaint smiles, they can transform the bravest of heroes into a fetal, whimpering ball. If you have trouble recruiting a demented clown, consider a hand puppet, marionette, or ventriloquist's dummy. Most any talking doll can be turned evil with a little effort.

computer programmers Not available until recently, the computer programmer is a new type of henchman, one that can help you control the information superhighway. Whether you need to hack the strategic defense computer, destroy the economy of Brazil, or just slash an innocent bystander's credit rating, these tech-savvy individuals are the ones to make it happen. After years at the keyboard, many computer programmers develop additional skills to leverage in support of your evil cause, such as blinding attackers with their sun-starved pallors and sending opposing ninjas reeling with one crack of their frighteningly oversized torsos.

winged monkeys These despicable minions have long served as henchmen for wicked witches, being naturally drawn to anyone in a pointy black hat with green skin. They serve as excellent scouts, scouring the land for young girls who happen to be wearing a pair of ruby red slippers. They can also make sinister soldiers, attacking from above in a fearsome wave of terror. Winged monkeys do have an unfortunate tendency to switch over to the other side, however, in particular when the protagonist has defeated you by throwing a bucket of water over your head. Consider them well for your army of darkness, but watch them carefully.

animal minions These denizens of the animal kingdom are an excellent choice for the evil-doer who has grown disenchanted with humanity. Instead of employing people, why not turn to rats, birds, snakes, feral cats, or whatever strikes your fancy? These purrfect beasts will serve as your eyes and ears in the beginning, then swell to horrific numbers and overrun the landscape later on. They also make great surrogates for the children you never had, inheriting the earth after you wipe out the plague that is humanity. If no one else understands you, animals make great friends.

mean english teachers These sadistic henchmen are perfect for when you want to inflict the greatest amount of pain possible. They are arrogant, humorless, and ridiculously strict, insulting their pupil's intelligence because they couldn't become writers themselves. They can extinguish any sense of creativity once held by an individual, as well as transform previously enjoyable literary works into nightmares of horror and confusion. Their monotonous tones are capable of driving even the sanest person to the brink of insanity, useful when you are in need of a torture master. Long after a child has grown up and become a hero, the sign of a mean English teacher continues to cause fear and discomfort.

The Mean English Teacher is perfect for when you want to inflict the greatest amount of pain possible.

What the undead lack in speed and agility, they more than make up for in persistence and can-do attitude.

the undead If you are an occult-minded evil-doer with access to the deceased, you're in a good position to use the undead as your henchmen. Through simple voodoo rituals and access to a town graveyard, you can raise up superpower-sized armies to serve as your fearless minions. The undead require very little maintenance and rarely demand a salary or benefits. What they lack in speed and agility, they more than make up for in persistence and can-do attitude. You won't hear any sass or whining from the undead! Since their victims are themselves transformed into walking undead, these henchmen are a smart investment that will grow your organization even when you're busy with other tasks.

corporate cronies Like lawyers, the business crony is great to have around to back you up, whether you're orchestrating a hostile takeover, practicing insider trading, defrauding the elderly of their savings, implementing gratuitous layoffs, or just engaging in routine blackmail and extortion. Heartless, frigid, and poised under pressure, the only drawback of corporate cronies is that they are prone to mutiny, thanks to their persistent ambition to seize power, even yours. Monitor their activities closely, and ready the pink slips should such the occasion arise.

supernatural creatures Dabblers in the black arts may wish to summon supernatural creatures to assist them in their evil deeds. Choose from gargoyles, demons, shambling creatures from beyond, or any of dozens of variations on the theme of mindless destruction. Notable for their superhuman strength and mystical powers, these monstrosities will serve your every need, provided you agree to help them fulfill their foul appetites. Unless they escape your control and eat you, supernatural creatures are a resource you can't do without.

Evil Hardware

At this point you may be saying to yourself, "I've got the lair, I've got the minions, now what?" Gentle evil-doer, this is the best part: choosing your weapons of destruction. If you plan to invent your own weapon, you can get started right away. If you're not sure what kind of weapon you want to use, peruse this list of favorites for ideas.

doomsday device If your goal is to destroy the world, then this is your weapon of choice. These weapons of mass destruction can be anything from hijacked nuclear bombs to molecular destabilizers to black hole generators. Their effect is fairly unimportant, because the purpose is always the same: complete and utter destruction of all life on Earth. Thus, only evil-doers who have chosen the "destroy the world" objective in their career life plan employ such devices. Use them first to extort heaps of cash from the governments of the world, and then go ahead and activate them after the ransom payment arrives. You are evil, after all, and an unused weapon is a terrible thing indeed.

book of evil What is an insidious occultist without a Book of Evil? These sorcery handbooks are conduits of unbridled power, so make it a priority to obtain one immediately. By mastering the dark within, you gain the ability to cloud men's minds, command the elements, and bring about terrible curses. You can also use the dark side to summon up demons, which is useful when you need a little mindless destruction. The only real problem with studying your Book of Evil is that weaker minds tend to go insane upon glancing at the contents. The unholy madness within seems to be just too much for some reason, and the weak almost always end up killing themselves. Rest assured that you are more than capable, however, and will succeed where they did not.

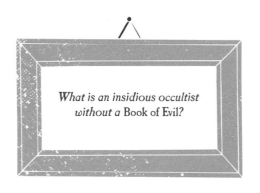

*What is an insidious occultist
without a* Book of Evil?

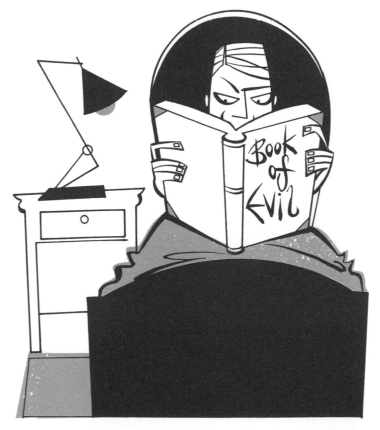

weather machine These amazing contraptions, long used by the evil community, are invaluable for holding small islands hostage. When you threaten to call down the power of a typhoon, the poor people of Naku Naku will have no choice but to hand over all their money and island women. You will find a number of environmental effects to choose from, including storms, thunder, lightning, monsoons, and even tsunamis. You can also use weather machines to attack larger nations, although you are usually confined to the destruction of the smaller coastal cities. Overall, they are a marvelous addition to any evil repertoire and will look impressive dominating the décor of your sinister lair. Just make sure you have enough room for them, as they tend to be really big with lots of levers and switches, pistons and lightning rods.

secret death ray Remarkably devastating and packed with sci-fi flair, secret death rays harness the power of the atom and unleash destruction like the world has never seen. They usually come in two forms: the handheld laser and the gigantic gun-thing. The first type is useful because it's so handy and portable. Should Flash Gordon try and interfere with your plans again, he will suddenly find himself nothing more than a heap of smoldering ash. The second option is also quite good, mostly in that it allows you to destroy armies, cities, and even planets. You will definitely require an incredibly large base for it though, at least the size of a small moon. Some sort of "Death Asteroid" or something.

grenades Supervillains should look into obtaining as many different types of grenades as possible. These delightful devices add an explosive element to any situation and are superb for localized destruction and quick escapes. You can obtain some flash grenades for stunning the enemy, poison-gas grenades for contaminating the ventilation system, and glue grenades in case you need to stop a tank in its tracks. Note, however, that any of these hand missiles require some degree of throwing skill. Evildoers plagued by poor athletic ability may wish to practice by throwing rotten eggs at passing vehicles, at least until their aim is of sufficient level.

These hand missiles require some degree of throwing skill.

unholy relics Be sure to add damned and cursed objects to your evil collection. A wide variety exists to choose from, ranging from sacrificial daggers and pagan idols to occult amulets of mystic might. Cursed swords and axes are also common, as are shrunken human heads and monkeys' paws. You can find most of these foul objects in forgotten tombs, although you may also have luck at an unholy shrine or plagued temple. After you have obtained a damned relic, you may notice your body start to change. Fur may sprout in unusual places, your fingernails may lengthen, and a tentacle or two may form. If you fondle your relic for a week or more without noticing any such changes, you inadvertently may have purchased or raided a *holy* relic. Discard immediately and bathe vigorously in the nearest certified quagmire.

Make Your Own Unholy Relics!

Most of those ornate relics you dream of possessing were handmade long ago by an evil craftsperson not so different from you. Why not make your own replica and have fun being creative at the same time? Try these ideas:

- Aluminum-foil crown of the doomed
- Bead-and-wire ring of fire
- Soap-dish forbidden voodoo idol
- Paper-towel-roll evil scepter
- Matchstick amulet of the damned
- Spooky-milk-carton votive-candle shade

Be sure to add damned and cursed objects to your evil collection.

matter transmuter If you happen to be a mad scientist or have one in your employ, then you might want to consider obtaining a matter transmuter. These wonderful devices were originally designed as short-range teleporters, but soon became useful for creating half-man monstrosities in the process. By simply shutting a victim inside with a fly, cat, or lizard, you can alter your dupe's DNA to unleash a scientifically spawned abomination never meant to exist on God's Earth. This transmogrification can be used as a punishment, to raise an army, to create that new look all the other evil-doers will rave about, or to vanquish a meddlesome hero. Imagine your most hated enemy trapped in a spiderweb screaming "Help me!" in a high-pitched voice. Delicious, isn't it?

time machine There is very little you cannot do with a time machine at your disposal. By transporting yourself to a different century or era you can learn valuable secrets, correct personal errors, and cause all manner of temporal mischief. Many evil-doers like trying to change history and will go back eight hundred years to alter some crucial event, or just to last Thursday to fix the botched bank job. Others elect to travel into the future to pick up some advanced technologies or to find out winning lottery numbers. The only real danger with using a time machine is running into a second version of yourself. Being evil, there is only room enough in this world for one of you, and you may have no choice but to destroy yourself.

Create that new look all the other evil-doers will rave about with a matter transmuter.

voodoo doll Another long-standing favorite, the voodoo doll is an excellent tool for malice and revenge. Through the mysteries of sympathetic magic, you can inflict horrific damage upon your enemies from afar, causing pain, impotence, and even death. You can also rip your enemy to shreds by simply placing the doll into a blender and punching frappé—good if you are feeling vengeful but don't have time for slow torture. Many different forms are available, ranging from the poppets of New England to crude stick figures used to frighten foolish campers. The main requirement is obtaining some bodily aspect of the victim, preferably hair or fingernails. Some evil practitioners find that a course or two at a beauty college gives them the skills they need to open a barbershop or nail salon downtown, thus ensuring a steady supply of potential voodoo victims.

invisibility potion The delight of evil-doers with a voyeuristic streak, and brewed by alchemists and mad scientists alike, the invisibility potion can render you incapable of being seen. One sip of this smoky concoction will allow you to travel where others cannot, learning valuable secrets and gathering an endless supply of blackmail material. You will have to remove your clothes in order to walk about, however, as disembodied suits rarely go far, but this is a minor inconvenience. That shortcoming directly relates to a larger problem, however, which is that duration tends to be inconsistent. Sad to say, more than one evil-doer has suddenly appeared au natural in the middle of a rival's board meeting or a female locker room. To avoid this situation, purchase your potion in bulk and experiment in the privacy of your evil lair until you have a good idea how long a dose from that particular batch will work its magic.

The voodoo doll is an excellent tool for malice and revenge.

This amazing technology will allow you to become a puppet master of millions.

orbital mind-control laser   One of the best contemporary methods for remote human manipulation, these space-bound satellites beam lasers directly into people's skulls and force them to obey your every command. This amazing technology will allow you to become a puppet master of millions, manipulating actions and emotions on a worldwide scale, with one exception. Should an individual wear a crudely fashioned aluminum-foil helmet, the laser beams will be deflected from their target. Luckily, only homeless people and conspiracy theorists have so far uncovered this simple but effective defense.

black army helicopters   The staple of any evil government or empire, a fleet of black army helicopters will serve your sinister needs well. Whether you need to deploy a team of jackbooted thugs or ferry enemies of state to your secret death camps, black helicopters are the way to go. They're dark, sleek, incredibly frightening, and the vehicle of choice among numerous evil agencies, so they boast plenty of negative connotations. Simply flying over in a black helicopter will make the huddled masses fear you, which can be a disadvantage if discretion is important. For better or worse, arriving in a black army helicopter sends a loud and clear message: "I'm important, and I'm evil." Most of these sinister copters are also equipped with advanced stealth technology for use on spy missions and other illicit operations.

toys of terror Irony is on your side when you manufacture and distribute specially modified games and toys. Not delightful playthings to inspire cheers on Christmas morning, these are vicious little invitations to terror. Start with a jack-in-the-box that attacks children, stuffed bears that come hungrily to life, and nutcrackers that quite disturbingly live up to their name. You can also create armies of toy soldiers, footballs that explode on contact, and board games that teleport their players to a parallel dimension. You might even create a Tickle Me version of yourself that devours souls instead of brain cells. Simply put, the world will be your toy chest, and none shall escape your kung fu grip.

Evil Fund Raising

Winged monkeys don't grow on trees, or at least not yet. If you're going to set yourself up as an evil magnate, you'll need cash and lots of it. Try these tips for landing cash fast:

- Evil bake sale or lemonade stand
- Evil paper route
- Arms sales to desperate nations
- Larceny, commissioned perjury, and extortion
- Day job as evil law clerk or accountant
- Telemarketing

Not delightful playthings to inspire cheers on Christmas morning, these are vicious little invitations to terror.

Fashion for the Evil-doer

I t is time now to deal with the most agonizing decision of your evil career. What to wear? How to display yourself? How to look "bad" and yet so damn good? It may seem wrong, but many people will form ideas about how evil you are based on how you dress and carry yourself. To make matters tougher, you'll want to look good while you are being bad. Read on for a variety of choices that will help alleviate the pain of this critical decision.

classic black It's hard to go wrong with classic black. Sinister, foreboding, fashionable yet fearsome, black creates an air of mystery while rendering you sneakier at night. It is also slimming, an important consideration if you are opting for a fitted style such as a cat suit or a cape and tights. Select high-saturation materials such as leather, velvet, and satin for the best effect. Your pasty white skin will shine with a hollow luminosity against head-to-toe black attire. Speaking of toes, black is really the only choice when it comes to evil footwear. Although many hero types and vigilantes now prefer black (thanks to years of trying to keep those white outfits clean), classic black remains *the* fashion statement for villains everywhere.

business suit The business suit is still the only real choice for corporate bastards and their cronies. Stick with a classic cut in gray, slate, charcoal, or navy. If you don't like wearing a tie, try pairing your suit with a black turtleneck or a silk T-shirt in charcoal. If you are accustomed to dressing on the cutting edge, you can try a statement suit with fashion features such as a high collar, four-to-six button tailoring, or man-made shiny fabric. Whatever style you choose, you are sure to feel a boost in confidence. When you put on a finely tailored suit, you know you look good and you'll enjoy the added benefit of making scruffier villains and heroes feel unkempt and out of place.

Black creates an air of mystery while rendering you sneakier at night.

supervillain costume with gimmicks   If you spent your childhood hiding in the backyard reading comic books, you probably won't be happy with anything less than the supervillain costume with gimmicks. Be it a green jumpsuit with question marks or an outlandish clown suit that shoots confetti, the gimmicky costume will bring contented smiles and automatically provide a motif from which you can adopt a personal theme. For example, I am the Lizard and use my tail-shedding weapon on you. As you design your costume, take your body type into consideration. Colorful leotards may be high on visual impact, but if it has been a few decades since your last trip to the gym, you may want to consider something with more coverage. Remember, spandex is a privilege, not a right.

robotic exoskeleton   Thanks to the innovative use of the robotic exoskeleton, the evil genius who was once frail and weak can now become an unstoppable juggernaut, gaining the strength of ten men and the durability of a tank. Machine guns and lasers can be attached to the sides and arms, and should your body ever be destroyed, your head can simply detach and rocket back to your underground lair. Regular lube jobs will keep the joints in your exoskeleton moving smoothly. Drawbacks include the potential for rust damage if you live in a moist climate and occasional problems getting served in public.

A gimmicky costume automatically provides a motif from which you can adopt a personal theme.

brain in a jar This option does not allow for as much mobility and personal interaction as the others do, but becoming a brain in a jar has been a favorite strategy among supervillains for decades. By suspending your brain in a slimy green goo, you can effectively cheat death and at the same time send the gross-out meter through the roof. Your henchmen will be incredibly confused and intimidated as you rant at them without any vocal cords, and your enlarged cerebral cortex will allow you to conceive of plans and schemes previously unfathomable. While you may not be able to enjoy your worldly assets anymore because of the absence of a body and any sensory organs, you will still be filled with wrath and rage, which is all an evil genius truly needs.

Becoming a brain in a jar has been a favorite strategy among supervillains for decades.

dominatrix outfit Female evil-doers often complain that the cat suit or studded bikini is their only option. Not so. The dominatrix outfit offers a feminine yet powerful look that exudes enthusiasm for the evil job at hand. Perfect for any lady of pain, the skin-tight garb is stain resistant and durable, making it a great choice for active evil-doers. You will find the complementary whip helpful for torturing heroes and the six-inch stiletto heels ideal for deadly jump-kick attacks. If you want to be feared, desired, and drop-dead gorgeous all in one, the dominatrix outfit is the look for you, although you may be a bit chilly at times.

battle armor Not surprisingly, miscreants engaged in the arts of war lean towards a wardrobe of battle armor. This formidable fashion can provide astonishing protection, allowing you to survive deadly assaults and what would normally be fatal blows. There are three types to choose from, determined by the era in which you exist. Medieval evil-doers prefer fine suits of plate armor, stylized with spiked helmets and menacing shields. Futuristic supervillains favor power armor, notable for its resilience and flight capability. Even criminal masterminds stuck in the present need not feel left out, given the nice array of ballistic armor and bulletproof vests currently available.

If you want to be feared, desired, and drop-dead gorgeous all in one, the dominatrix outfit is the look for you.

129

"*Wow, that really looks like blood.*"

wizard's robes Evil masterminds who possess a magical incli-
nation may want to invest their money in wizard's robes. These
sleek garments are ideal for sorcerers and necromancers alike,
providing fashion sensibility and open-air comfort. You can find
them in a wide range of colors, including soul-sucking black and
wow-that-really-looks-like-blood red, and they look great with
Grecian-style sandals or basic black supervillain boot-socks.
Avoid white wizard's robes, both because of the association with
good and because you will look like you're wearing a toga.

elemental Consider the possibility of constructing your body
entirely out of some sort of element. Earth, air, fire, and water
all make excellent forms, with individual benefits to each
(incredible toughness, ultraquick flight, devastating damage,
and ability to swim like a porpoise, respectively). They are not
the only choices, however, as you can also create a body out of
wood, metal, electricity, or even radiation (ideal for unstoppable
rampages). Glass is usually not recommended, as your jaw will
rarely last more than one punch. The big drawback here is lack
of publicity. As a disembodied wave wreaking havoc along the
coastline, you'll be at your peak of power, but no one will know
it's you. Your antics may even be chalked up to Mother Nature—
humiliating to say the least.

intelligence transferred into a computer This selection is quite similar to brain in a jar, only modernized and with more benefits. Through the act of transferring your intelligence into a computer you gain supreme power and access to information beyond your wildest dreams. Television cameras will act as your eyes and ears and robots your hands as you bring about great evil from twenty miles beneath the earth's crust. You will be effectively immortal, for transforming oneself into binary code tends to wrench away any last bits of humanity one might have. This is most definitely a good thing, as destroying the earth becomes that much easier.

wearing the skin of another human Perhaps you're not human at all, but rather a demon spawned from another world. Or maybe you're a necromancer, or someone who likes switching into other people's bodies. Whatever your story, you may want to try wearing the skin of another human. By concealing yourself in the flesh of your enemies you can constantly escape detection while committing countless evil acts. The different bodies will keep the authorities guessing, and when you get bored you can simply shed your current skin and move on to the next. There is also a great deal of fun to be had in tormenting heroes with this fashion. Consider, "Mom, is that you?"

Through the act of transferring your intelligence into a computer you gain supreme power beyond your wildest dreams.

The body double lets you become the mirror image of your goodly nemesis.

evil twin/opposite A wonderfully simple concept, the body double lets you become the mirror image of your goodly nemesis. Whether through the miracle of modern cloning technology or by being born into the role of evil twin, you are able to steal away a person's life and take it for your own. This works particularly well with heroes, as their friends will confide in you, purging their hearts of their deepest secrets. Your identical handprint and voice pattern will also allow you access to the securest of bases, providing further opportunities for espionage and frameups. If the hero you have become should ever catch up to you, he or she will be so flummoxed to see himself or herself looting the national treasury (or whatever you happen to be doing), they're likely just to stand there as you get away. The look on that hero's face should be worth any effort it takes to become their evil twin.

never revealing your face · This final possibility is perhaps best of all, as it allows the evil-doer to remain completely unseen to the outside world. Instead of being known by any particular name or gimmick, you are simply the mysterious force that no one ever sees but nonetheless knows exists because of the trail of destruction left in your wake. You become a kind of nightmarish monstrosity only hinted at in rumors and whispered about in folktales, existing out *there* somewhere, ready to eat your enemies should they get too close. The fact that no one ever sees you will only add to the legend, making you even more terrible and fierce. Furthermore, you can claim the evil deeds wrought by others to further your own reputation. People fear what they do not know, and though you may not actually even exist, you will be very fearsome indeed.

Give Yourself an Evil Makeover

Looking bad isn't just about your clothes. Spend a morning giving yourself an evil makeover and you may find you look horrendous in any outfit!

EVIL LOCKS ◄ Rat your hair, dye it jet black, and add a streak of silver down the middle. Or shave off all your hair, including your eyebrows.

NAILS OF THE DEAD ◄ Grow those nails long (longer!) or give yourself press-ons. Shape them into razor-sharp claws with a rusty blade and paint them green or tip them with red.

COMPLEXION CORRECTION ◄ Do you have that healthy glow? Fix it fast with green, blue, or white face paint.

POSTURE PERFECT ◄ Is your straight posture sending the wrong message? Slump and shuffle if you mean to be mean. Try contorting your hands and cocking your head for an exaggerated evil look.

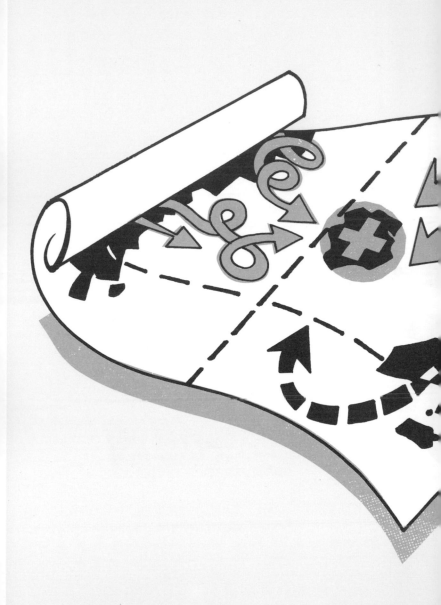

Chapter

V

Making an Evil Plan

"Go—and destroy in the name of DOOM."

— *Dr. Doom, Master of Latveria*

The Evil Plan Generator

Have you ever wanted to make a great evil plan but didn't have the time or superhuman intelligence? You're not alone. In fact, many evil men and women struggle with this culminating act in their trudge toward evil destiny. The secret to success is planning ahead. Use the following Evil Plan Generator to help you. By identifying your goals, means, and target for destruction, the Evil Plan Generator lets you concoct a truly nefarious scheme in a matter of minutes.

Simply fill in the blanks in each stage. When you are done, combine all three stages into a unique evil plan. We have offered some tentative suggestions for slow starters. Soon you'll unleash your sinister fantasy on an unsuspecting world as if you've been doing it for years.

Stage One:

To begin, you must first _____ _____ .
                                 Action   Target

Action: What are your favorite pastimes?

Kidnap
Clone
Devour
Blackmail
Incapacitate
Seduce
Expose
Incinerate

Target: What did you want to be when you were young?

A Police Chief
A Wealthy Heiress
A Military General
Superman
A Wizard's Apprentice
The Chosen One
A Town Mascot
A Rock Star

Stage 1 Continued:

This will cause the world to _____ , _____ by
your arrival.
                                  Reaction   Descriptive Verb

Reaction: What do people do when you enter a room?

Sit up and take notice
Swallow nervously
Choke on their food
Whisper among themselves
Sense a grave disturbance in the force
Sign up for life insurance policies
Slaughter a sacred calf to appease the gods
Leave

Descriptive Verb: How would you characterize the look on the doctor's face when you were born?

Amazed
Baffled
Shocked
Terrified
Frightened
Alarmed
Bewildered
Paralyzed

Wealthy Heiress

Military General

Rock Star

Stage 1 Continued:

Who is this _____? Where did they come from? And why do
          Name

they look so good in _____?
                        Fashion

Name: How would you describe yourself?

Criminal Mastermind

Evil Genius

Demented Madman

Right Bastard

Future Ruler of All Mankind

Bloodthirsty Warlord

Unholy Menace

Destroyer of All That Is Good and Nice

Fashion: What do you look best in?

Classic Black

A Business Suit

A Supervillain Costume

A Robotic Exoskeleton

Medieval Armor

Another Person's Skin

That Gigantic Silver Helmet

An Off-center Blond Wig

147

Stage Two:

Next, you must _____ _____ . This will all be done from
$\hspace{2.5cm}$ Action $\hspace{1cm}$ Monument

your _____ , a mysterious place of unrivaled dark glory.
$\hspace{1cm}$ Base

Action:
Seize control of
Disintegrate
Steal
Poison
Smash
Sabotage
Obliterate
Vaporize

Monument:
Mount Rushmore
Fort Knox
The Grand Canyon
The Pyramids of Giza
That Opera House in Sydney
The Internet
The Pacific Ocean
The Moon

Base: What is the location of your lair?
Medieval Castle
Corporate Tower
Underground Secret Headquarters of Doom
Desert Island
Abandoned Church
Ancient Tomb
Space Station

The Pyramids of Giza

The Moon

The Internet

Mount Rushmore

Stage 2 Continued:

Upon seeing this, the world will _____, as countless hordes of
                                       Reaction

_____ hasten to do your every bidding.
Henchmen

Reaction: How do mere mortals react to your presence?
Scream
Faint
Tremble
Give up
Weep uncontrollably
Gibber like madmen
Die in a way you just don't want to think about
Fall into catatonic trances

Henchmen: Who shall be your mindless slaves?
Corporate Cronies
Winged Monkeys
Robot Warriors
Ninjas
Alien Life Forms
Demented Clowns
Computer Programmers
The Undead

Stage Three:

Finally, you must _____ your _____ , bringing about _____ .
                    Action   Weapon   Destiny

Action:
Reveal to the world
Unleash
Covertly move
Release
Send forth
Let loose
Tauntingly wave
Activate

Weapon:
Corporate Takeover
Armies of Destruction
Doomsday Device
Secret Death Ray
Unholy Weapon
Needlessly Big Weather Machine
Armageddon Clock
Opening of the Seven Seals

Destiny: Your existence signals what?
The apocalypse
Horrors like the world has never seen
An end to sanity
Pain, suffering, the usual
A 1984-style police state
The return of the Antichrist
An unending cacophony of screams
Something really, really bad

Stage 3 Continued:

Your name shall become synonymous with _____, and no man

will ever again dare _____. Everyone will bow before your
                 Tragic Past

_____, and the world will have no choice but to _____.
Power   End Result

Random: Pick a word or phrase just for the heck of it.
Horror
Madness
All that is wrong with the world
Fuzzy bunnies

Tragic Past: What would no person ever do in your fearsome presence?
Beat you up
Call you names
Roll his or her eyes
Interrupt your sentences
Take your lunch money
Refuse to be your prom date

Power: What do you possess?
Supreme Might
Cunning Intelligence
Dashing Good Looks
Superior Firepower
Unmatched Physical Prowess
Mystical Abilities
Superhuman Powers

End Result:
Elect you dictator for life
Give you control of the planet
Send you all their money
Make you their new god
Name you Evil Man/Woman of the Year
Erect a gigantic statue of you
Restore your credit rating

HORROR

FUZZY BUNNIES

Blank Evil Plan for Handy Home Use

Having trouble flipping from page to page? Here is the Evil Plan Generator put together in shorthand for handy use at home. Simply fill in your answers in the appropriate blanks below and then get ready to call your press conference. You may want to photocopy this page first, in case you change your mind later and want to create a different evil plan.

Stage One:

To begin, you must first _____ _____. This will cause the
........................Action......Target

world to _____, _____ by your arrival. Who is this
.............Reaction....Descriptive Verb

_____? Where did they come from? And why do they look so
Name

good in _____?
...........Fashion

Stage Two:

Next, you must _____ _____ . This will all be done from
.....................Action....Monument

your _____, a mysterious place of unrivaled dark glory. Upon
.........Base

seeing this, the world will _____, as countless hordes of
.................................Reaction

_____ hasten to do your every bidding.
Henchmen

Stage Three:

Finally, you must _____ your _____, bringing about _____.
...................Action........Weapon.......................Destiny

Your name shall become synonymous with _____, and no man
....Random

will ever again dare _____. Everyone will bow before your
.....................Tragic Past

_____, and the world will have no choice but to _____.
Power...End Result

The world will erect a gigantic statue of you.

Sample Plan

Just to prove that it really does work.

Stage One:

To begin, you must first *kidnap The Chosen One.* This will cause the world to *sit up and take notice, shocked* by your arrival. Who is this *bloodthirsty warlord?* Where did they come from? And why do they look so good in *medieval armor?*

Stage Two:

Next, you must *seize control of that opera house in Sydney.* This will all be done from your *abandoned church,* a mysterious place of unrivaled dark glory. Upon seeing this, the world will *weep uncontrollably,* as countless hordes of *winged monkeys* hasten to do your every bidding.

Stage Three:

Finally, you must *unleash* your *doomsday device,* bringing about *horrors like the world has never seen.* Your name shall become synonymous with *madness,* and no man will ever again dare *call you names.* Everyone will bow before your *supreme might,* and the world will have no choice but to *erect a giant statue of you.*

Go Forth and Be Evil!

Think of your humble beginnings, when you dreamed of being bad or maybe terrible. Now you know better than to hold yourself back. Bad may have been good enough yesterday, but today you know who you are. You are evil. If anyone should accuse you of anything less than utter evil, just smile, knowing that proving you are evil isn't half as important as believing it yourself.